TRAINS

TRANSPORTATION

David and Patricia Armentrout

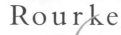

Rourke
Publishing LLC
Vero Beach, Florida 32964

www.rourkepublishing.com

PHOTO CREDITS: ©DigitalVision, LLC Cover, title page, pp.8, 15; ©Corel Corporation pp. 4, 7; ©Library of Congress p.10; ©Navets 17; ©PhotoDisc, Inc. p. 13; ©Transrapid p. 21; ©Wong p. 18.

Title page: *Eurostar passenger trains connect London to Paris and Brussels by traveling through the Channel tunnel.*

Editor: Frank Sloan

Cover design by Nicola Stratford

Library of Congress Cataloging-in-Publication Data

Armentrout, David, 1962-
  Trains / David and Patricia Armentrout.
    p. cm. — (Transportation)
Includes bibliographical references and index.
Contents: Trains — Early trains — American railroads — Freight trains — Amtrak — Famous trains — Subways — Commuter trains — Maglev trains.
  ISBN 1-58952-672-4
  1. Railroads—Juvenile literature. [1. Railroads. 2. Railroads—Trains.] I. Armentrout, Patricia, 1960- II. Title.   III. Series: Armentrout, David, 1962- Transportation.

  TF148.A66 2003
  385—dc21

                                                    2003007355

Printed in the USA

CG/CG

Table of Contents

Trains

A train is one or more cars that ride on wheels. A train travels along a track of double rails, called a **railroad**. The wheels of a train are grooved to fit over steel rails. The wheels glide smoothly across the rails, allowing heavy trains to move very fast along the track.

Trains can be pulled or pushed by an engine called a **locomotive**. Sometimes the locomotive is a separate car. Sometimes the engine is in part of a passenger car. Then it is **self-propelled.**

A locomotive pulls this passenger train.

Early Trains

The first locomotives were powered by steam. In 1804, an Englishman named Richard Trevithick built the first steam locomotive. Today, most trains are powered by a **diesel** engine or by electricity. Most electric trains collect power from overhead cables.

George Stephenson built the first public railroad in England in 1823. At first, the railroad hauled only **freight**. The railroad began carrying passengers in 1833.

The Jupiter *is a classic locomotive of the 1800s.*

American Railroads

Construction of railroads in the United States began in 1828. By 1848, America's East Coast had almost 6,000 miles (9,656 kilometers) of track. In 1869, a system of tracks met in Utah, forming an east-west connection. It was known as the **transcontinental** railroad.

The transcontinental railroad allowed people to travel long distances in comfort. Freight could be carried quickly over long distances, too. This railroad played a big part in the growth of many American cities.

Hundreds of freight cars wait to be unloaded at a rail yard.

Freight Trains

Freight trains haul cargo, just like the big trucks you see on our highways. The difference is that a freight train can haul as much cargo as 500 trucks.

Freight trains transport almost any product you can think of. For example, car manufacturers use freight trains to transport cars from factories to cities far away. In fact, 70 percent of all cars made in the United States are shipped by train.

American railroads grew rapidly during the 1800s.

Amtrak

Train travel became less popular in the early 1900s, mostly due to the invention of automobiles. In the 1960s, the rise of air travel also caused a decline in passenger rail service.

In 1971, the U.S. government combined the nation's railroads to create **Amtrak**. Amtrak increased passenger train travel.

Amtrak passengers ride in cars called coaches. A train that goes long distances may also have a baggage car, a dining car, and sleeping cars.

Amtrack runs more than 250 trains a day in 46 states.

Famous Trains

The Zephyr was a high-speed diesel train that began service in the 1930s. It holds a record for a sustained rail speed of 83.3 miles (134 kilometers) an hour on its Chicago-to-Denver run.

In 1964, Japan introduced its famous high-speed "bullet" trains. France introduced its TGV (Train à Grande Vitesse) high-speed trains in 1981. These electric passenger trains run at top speeds of 186 miles (300 kilometers) an hour.

Electric locomotives power TGV trains.

Subways

Subways are electric trains that run beneath busy city centers, such as London and New York. Subways provide fast transportation for a large number of people.

Passengers enter a subway from one of many stairways at street level. Subway cars have automatic sliding doors so passengers can enter and exit easily. Riders can sit in seats along the sides of the car or stand in the center aisle.

A subway is an underground railroad that provides fast transportation.

Commuter Trains

Many cities have commuter train service. Commuter trains take passengers around a city or to neighboring cities.

Some commuter trains run on elevated railways. Some elevated trains are monorails. Monorail trains have small wheels that "hug" a center track. Suspended trains are also elevated. Suspended trains hang below the railway, but travel above streets crowded with cars.

Elevated trains carry passengers on short commutes.

Maglev Trains

A train for the future is known as the "maglev." Short for magnetic levitation, these trains "float" on a cushion of air over a rail bed that has no tracks. Because the train floats, there is no **friction** caused by wheels moving along the track. The lack of friction enables maglev trains to travel up to 310 miles (500 kilometers) an hour. The world's first commercial maglev train is being tested in China and should begin operating soon.

A maglev train runs smoothly at a test site in Germany.

Dates to Remember

1804   The first steam locomotive is built by Richard Trevithick

1828   Construction of The Baltimore & Ohio Railroad begins

1833   England's first public railroad carries passengers

1869   Railroad tracks meet across the United States, forming the transcontinental railroad

1904   New York City opens its subway system

1964   Bullet trains are introduced in Japan

1971   Amtrak is created

1981   TGV trains are introduced in France

Glossary

Amtrak (AM trak) — the National Railroad Passenger Corporation created by the U. S. Congress; blending of the words "American" and "track"

diesel (DEE zuhl) — a fuel that is heavier than gasoline

freight (FRAYT) — goods or cargo carried by trains, planes, ships, or trucks

friction (FRIK shun) — a force that slows two objects when they are rubbed together

locomotive (loh kuh MOH tiv) — an engine used to pull or push railroad cars

railroad (RAYL rohd) — a track of double rails or the system of transportation that uses trains

self-propelled (SELF pruh PELD) — something that moves under its own power

transcontinental (trans kon tuh NEN tuhl) — crossing the continent

Index

Further Reading

Coiley, John. *Eyewitness: Train*. DK Publishing, 2000
Francis, Dorothy. *Our Transportation Systems*. The Millbrook Press, 2002
O'Brien, Patrick. *Steam, Smoke, and Steel: Back in Time with Trains*. Charlesbridge
    Publishing, 2000

Websites To Visit

www.amtrak.com/
www.rrmuseumpa.org/
www.sfmuseum.org/hist1/rail.html

About The Authors

David and Patricia Armentrout have written many nonfiction books for young readers on a variety of subjects. They have had several books published for primary school reading. The Armentrouts live in Cincinnati, Ohio, with their two children.